THE MIDDLE PASSAGE

WHITE SHIPS | BLACK CARGO

TOM FEELINGS

INTRODUCTIONS BY KADIR NELSON AND KAMILI FEELINGS

HISTORICAL NOTE BY Dr. SYLVIANE A. DIOUF

Dial Books *New York*

To my mother, Anna, and grandmother, Julia, whose powerful love insisted that
I was balanced enough to take on this challenge. To my friend, Andaiye, from Guyana,
who chose to enter the bowels of the slave ship with me, bringing her (old people's)
wisdom and patience, strengthening me for the long, lonely passage through the middle.
And finally to my lovely wife, Dianne, and our baby daughter, Niani Sekai,
my rewards, waiting for me, on this side of the journey.

T. F.

Dial Books
An imprint of Penguin Random House LLC
375 Hudson Street, New York, NY 10014

Art, and introduction on pg. 3 copyright © 1995 by Tom Feelings
Introduction, pg. 9 © 2017 by Kadir Nelson
Introduction, pg. 10 © 2017 by Kamili Feelings
Introduction, pg. 11 © 2017 by Sylviane Diouf

Printed in China
ISBN 9780525552444

1 3 5 7 9 10 8 6 4 2

Typography by Atha Tehon
Text set in ITC New Baskerville with Mantinia

The artwork was rendered using pen and ink and tempra on rice paper.
It was printed in tritone, using 2 black inks and one gray,
plus a neutral press varnish.

THE MIDDLE PASSAGE | TOM FEELINGS

Introduction to the Original Edition, 1995

The writer Paule Marshall once spoke of the "psychological and spiritual journey" that we must take back into the past in order to move forward. You have to engage the past, she said—to deal with it—"if you are going to shape a future that reflects you."

My personal journey started in the late 1950s, with drawing from my life in my own community in the streets of Brooklyn, New York, U.S.A., drawing all the faces and places I had seen most of my life but hadn't put down on paper until that point. I eventually took those developing skills to West and East Africa, the Caribbean islands, and finally to South America, physically tracing the trail from the motherland, Africa, through and into the diaspora—those places outside of Africa where black people now live. I was taking the "journey back in order to move forward."

Though I have been drawing and painting since I was a child, it was during the early 1960s that I became the most emotionally, spiritually, and creatively involved with depicting images of my own people. The Civil Rights Movement was sweeping America. Hundreds of thousands of black people were standing up, marching forward, refusing to be invisible. Outside of America, African and West Indian nations were fighting for independence. Since the 1954 and 1955 Supreme Court decisions that schools were to be integrated "with all deliberate speed," violence was being unleashed daily against any black people who tried to test the new law of the land. On television and in the newspapers, images flashed across the country of black Americas assaulted, beaten for trying to register to vote; small black children harassed by white mobs outside of schools; black churches being bombed in the South; black college students trying to desegregate "white only" sections of public stores. As time passed and the civil rights battle continued to heat up, all of these images—a mixture of pride, shame, anger, and despair—started moving into both my consciousness and my art, reflecting the frustration and sorrow of that period. I became concerned about a lack of balance in my work. As a black American I knew where the sorrow and pain came from, and it was beginning to overwhelm me personally. I wanted to know where the joy I felt, down deep, came from. Where did this joy originate?

So in 1964 I moved to West Africa. Africa. The original home of all black people. The country I chose to go to was Ghana. Ghana under president Kwame Nkrumah was in the forefront of the fight for African independence and a unified Africa. President Nkrumah welcomed the skills of black people from the Americas and the Caribbean. I lived and worked there for two years as an illustrator for the Government Publishing House. I did see the joy. Africa heightened my feelings of identity. For the first time in my life I was in the majority. I gained strength in my convictions, going out into the community of Accra, drawing all those places and faces my heart and eyes yearned to see and feel. Living in Africa reaffirmed much that was positive that I had deep inside me about black people. My drawings became more fluid and flowing.

Rhythmic lines of motion, like a drumbeat, started to appear in my work, and a style that incorporated a dance consciousness surfaced. My black-and-white paintings became brighter, the contrast glaring, a luminous glowing atmosphere of warm light set against and around dark skin. Even my colors became more vivid and alive, as though they possessed a light radiating from within.

Only once in Africa did the muted monochromatic somber colors of my art from America surface in my mind. One night while speaking with a Ghanaian friend, he asked quite unexpectedly, "What happened to all of you when you were taken away from here?" I knew instantly that he meant "what happened to all our people who were forcefully taken from Africa, enslaved, and scattered throughout the 'New World'?" He was referring to this crossing called the Middle Passage.

As he continued to speak, muted images flashed across my mind. Pale white sailing ships like huge white birds of prey, plunging forward into mountainous rising white foaming waves of cold water, surrounding and engulfing everything. Our ancestors, hundreds of them locked in the belly of each of these ships, chained together like animals throughout the long voyage from Africa toward unknown destinations, millions dying from the awful conditions in the bowels of the filthy slave galleys.

Is this what he wanted to know? Who could tell him this story with any kind of balance? Who would want to force himself emotionally into that horrible time to tell this story and risk the loss of sanity by stepping back into what has to be the most agonizing experience for any black person alive? Yet visually, for an artist, for a storyteller, what could be more challenging than this powerful, profound dramatic history, probing the memory, fueling the imagination, maybe even becoming a vehicle for creative growth? I began to see how important the telling of this particular story could be for Africans all over the world, many who consciously or unconsciously share this *race memory*, this painful experience of the Middle Passage. All of our ancestors, from so many different villages and regions of Africa, speaking different tongues, herded together into those miserable vessels, shared this horrible crossing of the waters.

But if this part of our history could be told in such a way that those chains of the past, those shackles that physically bound us together against our wills could, in the telling, become spiritual links that willingly bind us together now and into the future—then that painful Middle Passage could become, ironically, a positive connecting line to all of us whether living inside or outside of the continent of Africa.

I didn't answer my friend's question that night. Not in words. But unknowingly, he had started me thinking about how, in some form, I might be able one day to tell that story.

Nearly ten years would pass before this form would reveal itself to me. Within that period of time I returned to America, entering for the first time the newly integrated—one of the Civil Rights Movement successes—world of children's book publishing as an illustrator. For five years, with my main focus on African themes, I illustrated mostly picture books that I believed reflected my joy of living in Africa and projected that continent's heritage of celebration. My books emphasized the beautiful side of that black experience, especially for black children in America, who I knew were bombarded daily with negative texts and images of our ancient homeland.

In 1971 I was invited to the newly independent country of Guyana, the only English-speaking country in South America (formerly British Guiana, colonized by Holland and England, now populated by Africans who were imported and enslaved by the Dutch; by East Indians who were brought in by the British as indentured servants; and by Amerindians, the country's original inhabitants). This young third world republic of people of color rightly wanted to represent this majority by establishing a children's book unit within their ministry of education. I was brought in to train the local artists to illustrate texts written by the ministry's teachers. These texts and images were committed to telling the correct historical, painful truth to the children about how each group came to Guyana and who brought them there and why. A special emphasis was put on how they must now all work together to develop their new nation as free people. The project was designed to help the children *face* their history, straight on.

It was here, in this context, that I began to see that this was a form I could use. It could be a way of fulfilling my desire to show pain and sorrow as an unavoidable condition of black life, yet simultaneously to reveal the joy of that life's *rhythm* as an affirmation of the presence of life, all in a single project that used everything I had ever learned about the power of picture books. Storytelling is an ancient African oral tradition through which the values and history of a people are passed on to the young. And essentially I am a storyteller. Illustrated books are a natural extension of this African oral tradition. Telling stories through art is both an ancient and modern functional art form that enables an artist to communicate on a large scale to people young and old. I could use the form of historical narrative pictures telling a complete story to adults.

This would be my answer to that probing question posed to me by my Ghanaian friend in Africa years before. Enthusiastically I started reading everything I could find on slavery and specifically on the Middle Passage. I searched out and wrote down all of the factual incidents in sequential order, reading some personal accounts by former slave-ship captains, slave traders, and various European historians. I expected the descriptions of the horror of the slave forts and the inhuman treatment on the journey aboard the slave ships. But some of the writers' overbearing opinions, even religious rationalizations and arguments for the continuance of the slave trade made me feel, the more words I read, that I should try to tell this story with as few words as possible, if any. Callous indifference or outright brutal characterizations of Africans are embedded in the language of the Western World. It is a language so infused with direct and indirect racism that it would be difficult, if not impossible, using this language in my book, to project anything black as positive. This gave me a final reason for attempting to tell the story through art alone. I believed strongly that with a picture book any African in this world could pick up and see and feel what happened to us on those ships. I also wanted these images to have a definite point of view and the *passion* in them that reflected clearly the experience of the people who endured this agony. But I couldn't get the artwork started in South America. Finally I realized I had to be in a place that constantly reminded me of what I was working on and why I was working on it. For me, that was New York City. That's where the pain was.

I moved back to America. It took me two years and six months to finish the preliminary drawings. I didn't know when I started this project that time was the essential thing I needed to tell the story completely in pictures—the kind of time one associates with the form of a long novel. Time for me to open myself up and explore the mind not just of one single person going through this experience, but the minds of a whole people. A people who lived and still live this story with all its complex social and historical implications through the diaspora. A phrase began to form in my consciousness, one that I have often used to describe the creation of this story in pictures: "The pain of the present sometimes seems overwhelming, but the reasons for it are rooted in the past."

And as time went on, as painful as it was to force myself each time back into the agonizing past, it was equally as painful to come back through history, hoping for relief, only to see some of the same things in the present, in America, the richest country in the world . . . hundreds of the city's poor eating out of garbage cans; thousands of homeless people, young and old, across the country living in the streets; and tens of thousands of "middle class" people, black and white, on unemployment rolls . . . reminding me that a part of America's legacy is the killing off of most of its original inhabitants and importing against their will enslaved Africans to work the land, using the rationalization of skin color to continue it for centuries. A government that tolerated the dehumanization of human beings in its infancy and for such a long period of time is capable of tolerating it in the present. I was seeing the results of slavery, reminding me constantly why I was working on this project.

Still I felt the need for another kind of feedback. So for the first time in my life I let people—black people—come into my studio and look at the work in progress. I watched their faces as they went from drawing to drawing, turning page after page in sequence. All kinds of people, young and old. I listened as they voluntarily opened up and told me about the joyful and the sorrowful things in their lives. And I began to soak up all this information. All those stories, all those things that as one person I could never experience in a single lifetime. Then when I was alone I let it seep slowly into all of my art. Years passed. I began to become uncomfortably aware of the fact that a lot of time had passed, and I was far from finished. In some cases I had to keep doing some paintings over and over until the mood was right . . . exactly right. Then and only then could I move on to the next one, sometimes trying to force the process by painting two at the same time. It wouldn't work. Sometimes overly tired, I'd tell myself that I needed sleep, trying to move away from the whole thing.

But in my feverish half-sleep my deceased maternal grandmother would come to me and say, "Get up, go back to it, and start over again . . . because you are not doing this just for yourself." My friends and others began to question why this project was taking so long. But I couldn't work any faster. Then one night I sat down and thought about all those artists and writers that I truly respected, like John O. Killens, Margaret Walker, Charles White, Paule Marshall, John Biggers . . . the ones who took the time, a long time, to finish their work in the only way they could . . . in their best way, even when it meant staying on the edge for long periods of time. And that calmed my fears.

It is almost twenty years later. I have finished this long "psychological and spiritual journey back in order to move forward" with the completion of the last painting in *The Middle Passage*—a story that has changed me forever. My struggle to tell this African story, to create this artwork as well as live creatively under any conditions and survive, as my ancestors did, embodies my particular heritage in this world. As the blues, jazz, and the spirituals teach, one must embrace all of life, both its pain and joy, creatively. Knowing this, I, *we*, may be disappointed, but never destroyed.

It has been more than twenty years since I opened Tom Feelings's powerful book *The Middle Passage* for the first time. I remember walking into a book store and seeing it prominently displayed on the bookshelf. It seemed to draw me closer and compel me to pick it up and have a look.

At the time, I was a senior at Pratt Institute studying illustration, and I began to seriously contemplate my future as a working artist. A career in children's publishing wasn't even a thought just yet. I only knew I wanted to create impactful paintings that told the stories of African American people. It was no coincidence that I'd be drawn to Feelings's incredible book. His artwork was exactly what I needed to see in that moment.

I opened the pages to find haunting black-and-white images detailing the harrowing journey of millions of Africans and Europeans whose lives collided to shape what would be known as the Transatlantic West African slave trade. Aside from a preface by the author and the original introduction, by John Henrik Clarke, there were no words printed along with the interior artwork. They weren't necessary. Each powerful image spoke volumes. Men, women, children, captives, captors, yearning, crying, fighting, trying to escape the inescapable. Feelings's soft pastel and charcoal black-and-white drawings were moving, visceral, and intensely emotional, with great spiritual integrity. They were ghostly, ghastly, powerful. The images stayed with me long after I turned the last page.

I was not aware of it then, but in a few short months I'd be hired as a visual development artist for the feature film *Amistad*.

At the time, there was no director assigned to the film, and one of the film's producers, Debbie Allen, and production designer Rick Carter were looking for artists to create imagery to inspire director Steven Spielberg to take on the film. I was charged with illustrating key moments in the story, namely, scenes that visually described the Middle Passage. We were provided an abundance of photographic reference detailing life in West Africa and all things related to the Middle Passage. During a meeting with Ms. Allen, she showed images from Feelings's book to induce us to understand the emotional, physical, and psychological trauma of the weeks-long, sometimes months-long journey across the ocean. Until *The Middle Passage* was published more than twenty years ago, there had never been an intimate visual history of the Middle Passage of this magnitude or in this format.

In *The Middle Passage*, the artist employed two very important choices to tell the story. The first was an elegant palette consisting of only black and white, a choice that mirrored the brash oversimplification of reality: The obvious truth that the identities of African peoples—Ashanti, Mandingo, Mende, Temne, Ibo, Fulani, and others—and those of the Europeans—Portuguese, French, British, Spanish, and Dutch—were distilled and blurred into merely Black and White. "White ships, Black cargo."

Secondly, the artist's choice to utilize a wordless format was brilliant. Any attempt to describe the traumatic experience of the Middle Passage always falls short. There simply are no words that accurately condense the experience into mere syllables. Instead, the artist relied on the power of the imagery to communicate the unspeakable. Every one of Feelings's sixty-four works of art tells an essential part of the story from beginning to end. The attention to detail is impressive. Feelings's remarkable offering recalls the masterful works of painters like Francisco de Goya, John Biggers, Charles White, and Leo and Diane Dillon. Ultimately, Feelings's compositions and this incredible twenty-year labor of love is unlike anything else.

Today, as I study each brilliant image, I am struck with even greater appreciation for this volume. Feelings's visual narrative inspires us to revisit the conversation about this shameful part of American history. It is a beautiful and purposeful work of brilliant design, brave artistic choices, elegant compositions, laborious technique, and dedication. A provocative life's work that never gets old. I respectfully tip my hat to Mr. Tom Feelings, a masterful artist and storyteller.

THE MIDDLE PASSAGE | INTRODUCTION BY KAMILI FEELINGS

During the last ten years of his life, my father, Tom Feelings, shared a lot of his life story with me; that period of transparency, about both his life and his work, turned out to be one of the greatest gifts that he ever gave me. By the end, we could share a laugh together as easily as any lifelong friends. He had shown extraordinary patience and focus in his lifetime—in fact, I couldn't have pictured having that level of connection with him when I was younger, as my father had always seemed far too busy to slow down. In addition to illustrating many other books, he spent thirty years of his life designing, drawing, and hand-painting the sixty-four pieces of black-and-white artwork that would eventually become this book, *The Middle Passage: White Ships, Black Cargo.* By 1995, when it was published, from conception to completion, this "picture book" was older than I was.

My years-long conversation with my dad about *The Middle Passage* began in 1996. I sat quietly and listened to him speak about some of the dilemmas he faced in trying to paint this epic narrative. Some of the heavier content especially made him feel, after prolonged exposure, alone and overwhelmed. Some of the more stunning, abstract paintings in the book, in fact, would emerge out of the plain *impossibility* he would feel, around the task of depicting the entirety of the slave trade in a limited number of illustrations.

Even after completing this work, my father felt compelled to return to the subject of the slave trade again and again. *The Middle Passage* grew and evolved into something larger than a book project for him; long after the book's publication, my father continued to process its meaning. He felt compelled to seek out and engage with criticisms of the book. He saw no shame in revising his understanding of the subject matter; in fact, he felt that being constantly in conversation with critics allowed him to grow as an artist and as a storyteller.

I feel honored to have been able to discuss some of my father's biggest questions about his life's work with him. Had he focused too much on men's stories in *The Middle Passage?* Could he have included more women in the narrative? (In one particularly provocative illustration, a tortured [or enraged] female figure, engorged with a slave ship for a belly, hurls herself through murky and frothy waters. *Where is she headed? And whom will her wrath touch down upon?*) And what about the ways *The Middle Passage* reflects enslaved peoples' resistance? (The book renders mass suicide as complicated and bittersweet, a form of heroic dignity in the face of tyranny. *How did they cast themselves so confidently into the ocean?*) How does their resistance mirror the struggles of their descendants throughout American history?

As you begin to read this book, my father's talent will be self-evident. I hope I've also given you a notion of his sense of responsibility as an artist. My dad truly desired to get his art projects "right." And this meant continuing to engage with them, even long after they were complete.

THE MIDDLE PASSAGE | A HISTORICAL NOTE BY DR. SYLVIANE A. DIOUF

When he disembarked from the slave ship that had taken him from Benin to Brazil, Mahommah Gardo Baquaqua recalled, "I felt thankful to Providence that I was once more permitted to breathe pure air (…) I cared but little then that I was a slave, having escaped the ship was all I thought about." Baquaqua was one of 12.5 million Africans to endure the horrific Middle Passage between 1501 and 1867. And he was one of only 10.7 million to survive it.

The transatlantic slave trade was the largest forced migration in history, and it started with gold fever. For a long time, Muslim North Africans had traded with West African Muslim kingdoms and empires south of the Sahara for their gold, ivory, and pepper, part of which the North Africans sold to the Europeans. But Portugal wanted to directly access the gold as well as the Sub-Saharan populations in the hope of mounting a new crusade against the Muslims. The venture would be financed with African gold, and some of the troops would be Africans forced to convert to Catholicism. The Portuguese reached Senegal in 1444, and by 1483 they had sailed south to the Congo River. Everywhere they went, they kidnapped people and met with fierce resistance.

For centuries, Europeans had enslaved their own. Like the various peoples who lived in Africa, the diverse populations in Europe did not share a common identity as Europeans. They did not see themselves as "white," just like people in Africa did not see themselves as linked by the color of their skin. By the fifteenth century, grouped under the term *Slavs*—a term that gave rise to the word *slave*—European slaves were mostly Russians, Bulgarians, Albanians, Bosnians, and Greeks. West Africans, first introduced to Europe by North Africans, were a minority of the enslaved population. Two major events changed the situation. First, when the Muslim Ottoman Turks seized Christian Constantinople in 1453, they redirected the supply of European slaves to their empire in the Middle East and North Africa, and Sub-Saharan Africans replaced enslaved Europeans in Portugal, Spain, and Italy.

The second event was the conquest of the Americas, starting in 1492. The first Africans sent to the "New World" came from Spain and Portugal and gradually replaced enslaved Native Americans, who had been decimated by new diseases and wanton massacres.

With the discovery of gold and silver and the introduction of sugarcane, Africans entered the Americas directly from Africa starting in 1525. Brazil, Portugal, Great Britain, France, Spain, Denmark, Sweden, the Netherlands, and the United States organized and benefited from this massive deportation. From 1701 to 1800—the peak of the slave trade—6.5 million Africans crossed the Atlantic and 5.6 million reached its western shore. By 1820, Africans represented 80 percent of all the people headed for the Americas.

Africans responded to the onslaught with a variety of strategies. People attacked slave pens and ships, which led slave dealers, wherever possible, to locate the slave pens (also called factories and barracoons) on islands or in forts to prevent assaults and escapes. To defend themselves, their communities, and their states, African people bought firearms from the Europeans, who only accepted captives in exchange. It is estimated that by the end of the eighteenth century 20 million guns and 22,000 tons of gunpowder had been shipped to Africa. Africans also traded captives for iron—there was limited quantity in West Africa—which they used to forge still more weapons. Some people were thus taking part in the slave trade as they tried to defend themselves from it; others—mainly the political and commercial elite—were motivated by greed.

As a long-term defensive strategy, communities relocated to hard-to-reach areas. They built their villages and town as mazes to disorient attackers, surrounded them with thick walls and deep ditches to keep invaders out, or established new homes close to forests or the sea to facilitate escape. When all else failed, families who could find relatives being held on the coast bargained for their release, but slave traders demanded two or more individuals in exchange for each captive. People had to choose: They could kidnap strangers or see their loved ones disappear forever in the holds of the ships heading to the Americas.

The Middle Passage was how Europeans referred to the second leg of the so-called triangular trade that linked Europe to Africa and the Americas. The first leg of the triangular trade started in European ports with ships transporting goods to be exchanged for captives in Africa; the second leg was the crossing of the Atlantic Ocean from Africa to the Americas with the captives on board; the third leg was the journey from the Americas back to Europe with the ships loaded with the cotton, sugar, rice, tobacco and other raw material produced by slave labor.

The so-called Middle Passage was "middle" only for the Europeans; for the Africans it was the first segment of an immensely tragic overseas journey into a future none of them could have imagined. But before they even set foot on the ships, they had already gone through the harrowing experience of several land-based "passages." Villagers and city dwellers, soldiers, deposed rulers, farmers, traders, herders, fishermen, artisans, Islamic schoolteachers and students, and religious leaders became prisoners of war, refugees, and victims of kidnapping or raids. Others were convicted of real or made-up crimes. Europeans called them slaves, but until they were sold in the Americas, Africans considered themselves captives or prisoners. After walking to the sea—which for some could take several weeks—they were confined to seedy factories where they spent weeks or months as traders endeavored to fill their ships. Captives were routinely branded. Baquaqua and his companions were "ordered not to look about us, and to insure obedience, a man was placed in front with a whip … another man then went round with a hot iron, and branded us the same as they would the heads of barrels or any other inanimate goods or merchandize."

When the time of departure arrived, families and friends were torn apart. Depending on the buyer, some would end up in Jamaica, while others would spend the rest of their lives in Colombia or Panama. Cudjo Lewis, who, along with 109 children and young adults, left Benin on the *Clotilda*—the last slave ship to reach the United States in July 1860—recalled how much they cried that night because they did not want to leave their friends and relatives in the barracoon and because they longed for home and did not know what was going to happen to them.

As the captives were led to the shore, Ottobah Cugoano, who was thirteen when he was deported from Ghana to Grenada, described what happened on the beach. "[I]t was a most horrible scene; there was nothing to be heard but the rattling of chains, smacking of whips, and the groans and cries of our fellow-men. Some would not stir from the ground, when they were lashed and beat in the most horrible manner."

A deeply humiliating and traumatic ritual awaited men, women, and children as they boarded the ships. "The people of the great vessel were wicked," Ali Eisami of Nigeria remembered, "when we had been shipped, they took away all the small pieces of cloth which were on our bodies, and threw them into the water." According to slave dealer Theophilus Conneau, "This precaution is necessary to keep them free from vermin." In fact, the forced nakedness did nothing to alleviate the filthiness of the slave ships that crawled with lice, fleas, mice, and rats. The fear that people could hide weapons under their clothes or use them to hang themselves was at the root of this degrading measure.

Approximately half of the ships that traveled the Middle Passage carried between 100 and 300 captives, but thousands of the vessels crammed from 500 to 700 people into their holds. In 1852 one thousand people from Mozambique crossed the ocean on the *Rapida Emperatriz*. The 840 survivors disembarked in Cuba. About seven out of ten African captives were males. The adults were always shackled, one to the other by the wrist and leg, and the shackles caused excruciating blisters and open sores. They lay on platforms like books on a shelf, stated slave captain John Newton, author of the famous hymn "Amazing Grace." Some ships had two platforms with five feet or less between them. Because of their shackles, Newton acknowledged, it was "difficult for [the men] to turn or move or attempt to rise or lie down without hurting themselves or each other." Some ships had three shelves, each built about nineteen inches from the other. The movements of the ship sent them violently bumping into one another. An African American whose grandfather crossed the Atlantic and was sold in Mississippi told him that during storms, some people hit their heads against iron bars and died. Women and children under fifteen were rarely fettered and were held at the back of the ship separate from the men. Slave captains admitted that crews often abused them. Cugoano was indignant: "It was common for the dirty filthy sailors to take the African women and lie upon their bodies." Women cooked the captives' meals, and the sailors often used them and the children as domestics.

For all, the heat and the thirst were unbearable. Below deck temperatures could reach 130 degrees. Steam from the bodies came up through the gratings "like a furnace," testified a slave ship captain. Cudjo and his companions received a mouthful of water twice a day. Rain was welcome: They caught the drops in their hands and mouths. Confined under deck where he could not stand up, Baquaqua remembered, "day and night were the same to us, sleep being denied us from the confined position of our bodies, and we became desperate through suffering and fatigue. . . . I suffered, and so did the rest of us, very much from sea sickness at first, but that did not cause our brutal owners any trouble." Olaudah Equiano from Nigeria wrote, "the air soon became unfit for respiration, from a variety of loathsome smells, and brought on a sickness among the slaves, of which many died (…) This wretched situation was again aggravated by the galling of the chains, now become insupportable; and the filth of the necessary tubs, into which the children often fell, and were almost suffocated. The shrieks of the women, and the groans of the dying, rendered the whole a scene of horror almost inconceivable." For thirteen days, Cudjo and his friends remained confined to the hold. When they were allowed on deck, the crew had to carry them, as they could not stand up and walk on their own. On most ships it was customary to bring the captives up on deck, where they were forced to "dance." This was another humiliating ritual that forced naked men and women to jump up and down. To the men, loaded with heavy shackles, the "healthy exercise" was a torture.

The misery of their physical condition was but one aspect of the captive Africans' ordeal. The loss of their freedom, their old life, and their loved ones was what distressed them the most. According to one slaver, people became "sick, sometimes owing to their crowded state, but mostly to grief for being carried away from their country and friends." William Thomas from Cameroon shared memories of his companions' suffering: "All cried very much at going away from their home and friends, some of them saying they would kill themselves." Dr. Trotter, a physician, attested that Africans "showed signs of *extreme distress and despair, from a feeling of their situation at being torn from their friends and connections.*" At night he could hear them make "a howling melancholy noise, expressive of extreme anguish." A woman who served as an interpreter told him it was because they had dreamed "they were *in their own country again,*" and found as they woke up that they were on the slave ship. To the surprise of crews, despite their desperate situation, Africans sang. But their songs, as the Europeans soon learned, "were songs of sad lamentations," one slave ship physician explained, "they were all sick, and by and by they should be no more; they also sung songs expressive of their fears of being beaten, of their want of victuals, particularly the want of their native food, and of their never returning to their own country."

With so many people living in indescribable filth, underfed, and dehydrated, epidemics quickly spread. Dysentery, malaria, yellow fever, scurvy, measles, and smallpox were the main causes of mortality. On the *Elizabeth*, 155 people out of 602—one in four—died. On average, about 15 out of every 100 Africans—close to two million men, women, and children—perished and were thrown overboard, making the Atlantic Ocean an immense graveyard. They mostly died from various illnesses, but also from suicide and from being shot, hanged, tortured, or thrown into the ocean during insurrections. Resistance took several forms; the most common was suicide, either through hunger strikes or drowning. Those who refused to eat were flogged; their mouths were forced open and food was pushed down their throats. When Equiano stopped eating, he was brutally whipped. He wrote, "Could I have got over the nettings, I would have jumped over the side, but I could not; and, besides, the crew used to watch us very closely . . . lest we should leap into the water: and I have seen some of these poor African prisoners most severely cut for attempting to do so, and hourly whipped for not eating." To prevent suicide by drowning, ships were surrounded by nettings.

With shackles, iron collars, manacles, and chains hobbling the men; dozens of sailors armed with guns, ropes, and whips; and cannons at the ready, insurrections were extremely difficult to organize. Yet, they happened on one in every eight or ten ships, and women and children were instrumental in many. Going and coming on deck, they knew the crews' routine and where the weapons were held, and they often communicated with the men through songs. On Cugoano's ship, "It was the women and boys which were to burn the ship, with the approbation and groans of the rest." The women on the *Tryal* sang loudly to cover the sailors' screams as the men started to kill them in the ship's holds. In 1773, onboard *New Britannia*, the men cut their way through the bulkhead with the tools the boys had given them. They seized guns and fired on the crew. When they realized they were losing the battle, they blew the ship up with 236 captives and 53 crew-members on board. Africans on the *Unity* started a revolt on June 6, 1770. It was crushed, but they tried again on three separate occasions. Their objective was to kill the crew and, if unsuccessful, to jump overboard. If impeded by their shackles, they were determined to burn the ship down. Revolts occurred on the African shores, in the middle of the ocean, or close to the American coasts. One successful uprising happened in 1800 at the point of arrival. The Senegalese on board the *San Juan Nepomuceno* forced the first officer to take them from Uruguay to Senegal, where they arrived several months later.

Depending on the ship and the place of departure and arrival, the crossing of the Atlantic could take 30 to 130 days. People landed in terrible shape: weak, bruised, sick, injured, infected. Often unable to walk, they had to be carried off the ships. Many of those who landed in Uruguay and Argentina had to endure a second voyage, this time on foot, through plains and snow-covered mountains to the mines of Bolivia and Peru two thousand miles away. Among the survivors of the British slave trade, over 300,000 quickly boarded new ships that transported them from the Caribbean to North America, from one island to another, or from British settlements to Spanish or French colonies. Still, throughout the Americas, resourceful newly arrived Africans were prompt to run away. In 1759, Arrow escaped two days after landing in South Carolina. Despite being in an unknown environment, he remained hidden for years. Samba ran away five days after he arrived from Gambia in Annapolis, Maryland. Another Gambian who disembarked in South Carolina, was gone a month later with shackles on his legs, which means that he had already run away and been caught once.

Leaving the ship was all Baquaqua thought about during the journey, but it was also traumatic. When three young girls who had just disembarked in Charleston, South Carolina, were separated, "they threw themselves in each other's arms . . . They hung together and sobbed and screamed and bathed each other with tears," recounted a witness. "At parting, one of the girls took a string of beads with an amulet from her neck, kissed it, and hung it on her friend's." In the midst of unimaginable suffering, Africans for whom family and community were so crucial had re-created on the ships the close-knit families they had lost. This new community was made of people of various ethnicities, languages, religions, and former social status. Although the Middle Passage has become synonymous with the Africans' dreadful journey, the word that to them best captured their experience was "ship." The ship was the place of unspeakable hardship and it was also the place of unbreakable kinship. The shared ordeal had forged a special connection. Captives called one another ship-mates in Jamaica, *batiments* in Haiti (*ship* in French), *malungo* and *malongue* in Brazil and Trinidad (from the Kikongo phrase "in the ship"), *sippi* in Suriname (from the Dutch *schip*), and *carabela* in Cuba (*ship* in Spanish). These words have endured. They are still used today by African descendants to express a relationship not based on bloodlines.

From the depth of the slave ship, a culture of community and resistance emerged. The malongue, the sippi, and the shipmates formed new communities in the hell of the mines and the plantations; they built autonomous lives in the mountains and the forests; and they organized uprisings from New York to Bahia. Millions of Africans brought with them their cultures, languages, knowledge, and religions, and created new languages, new cultures, new knowledge, and new religions. Their agony was unspeakable and yet their resilience, determination, and creativity were instrumental in the creation of a world that has not properly acknowledged and celebrated their invaluable contribution.

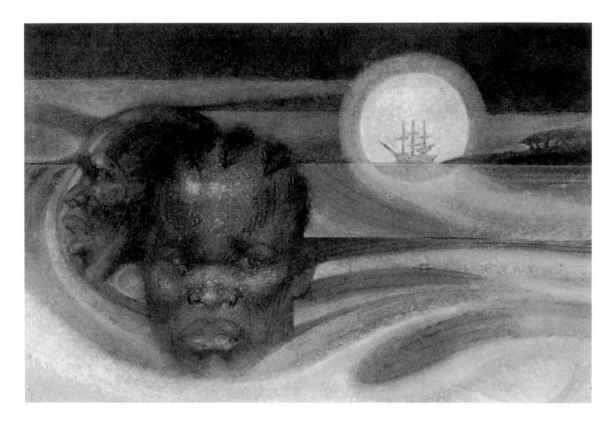

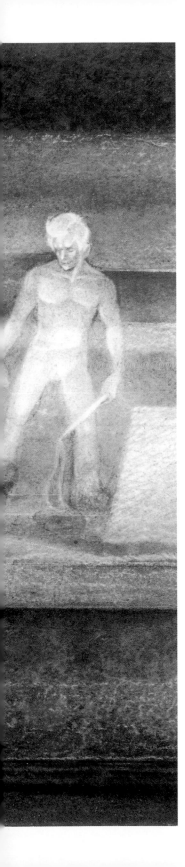

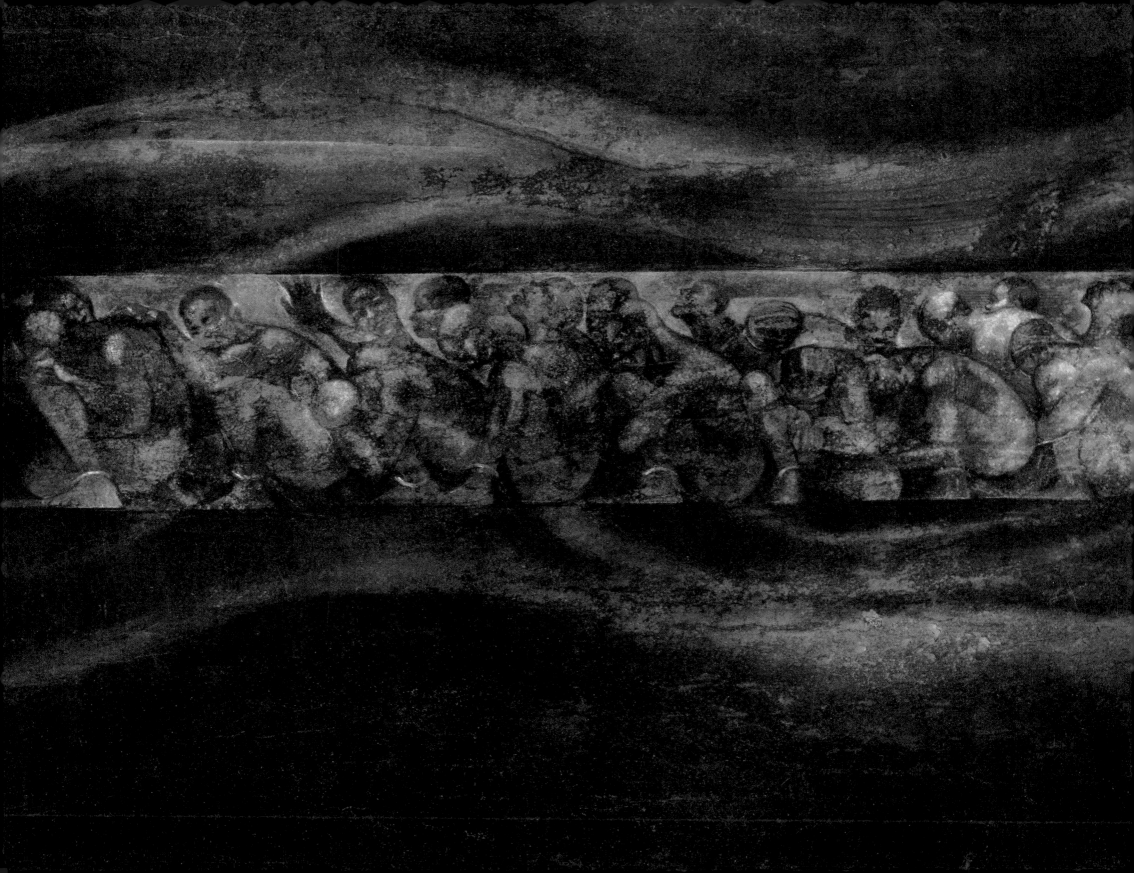

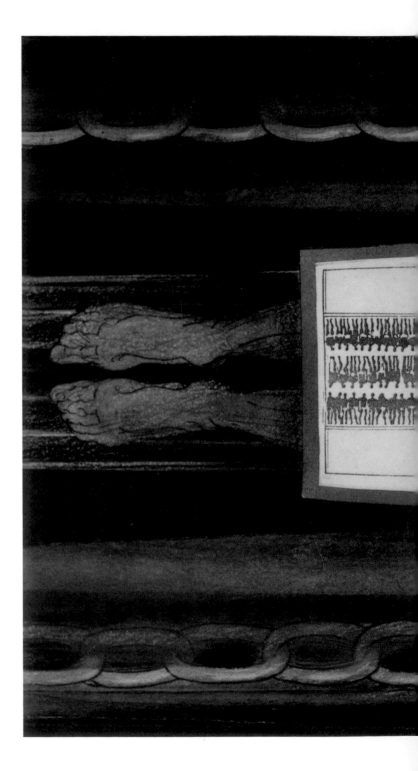

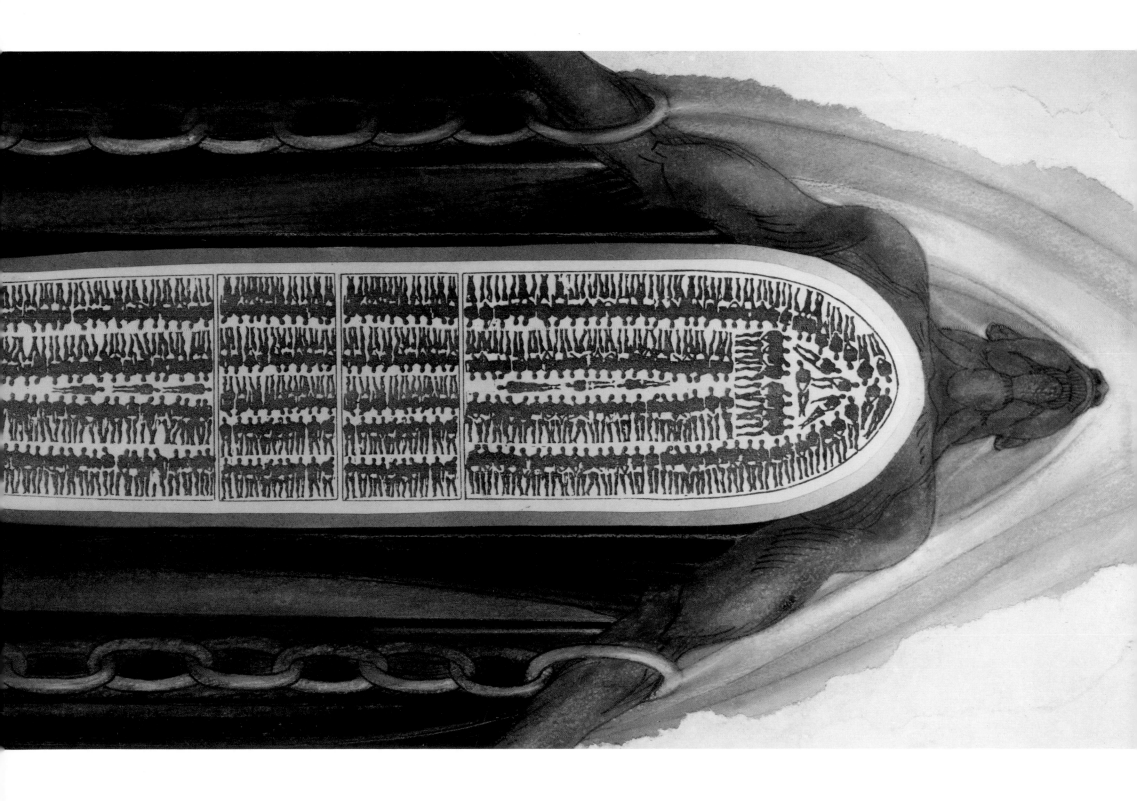

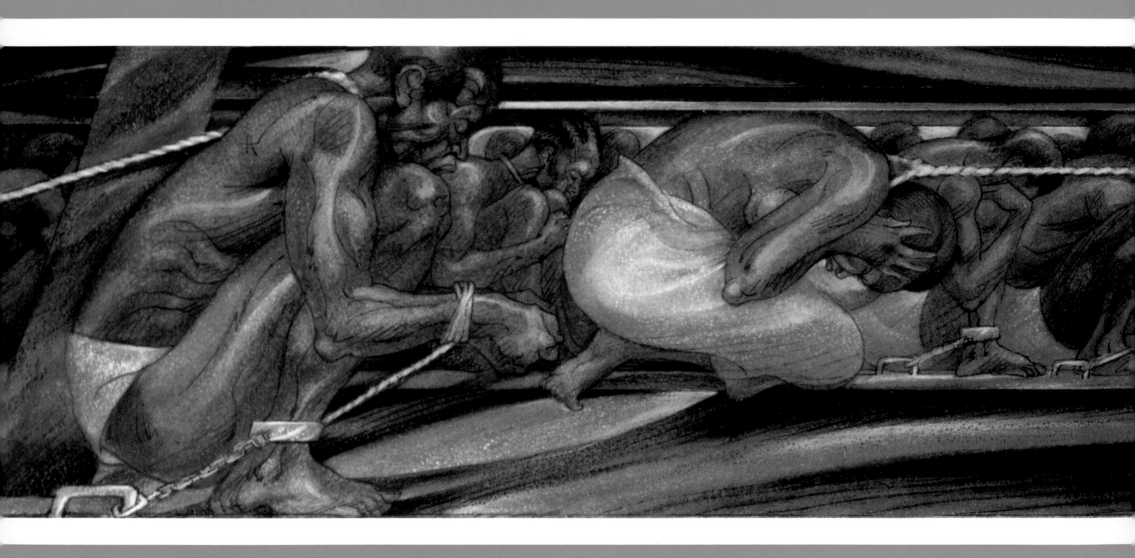

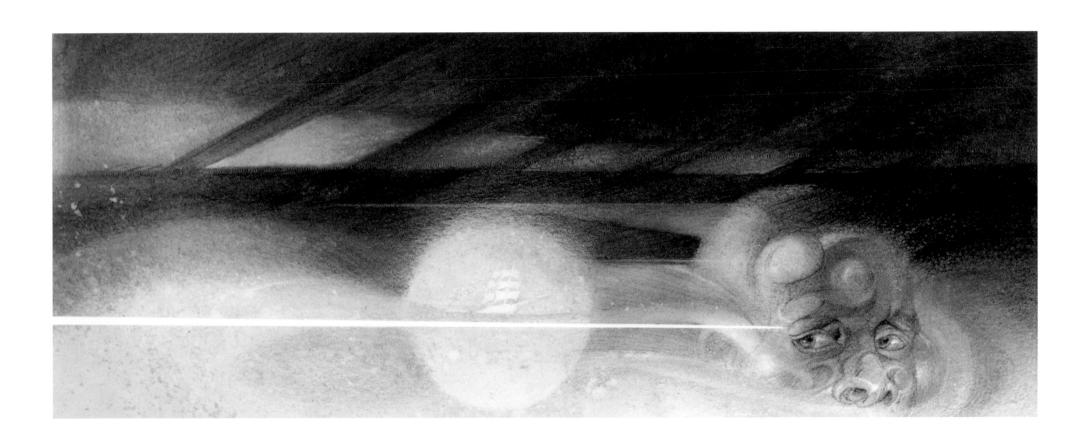

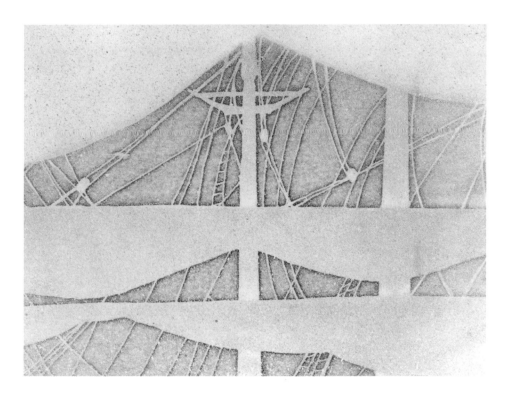

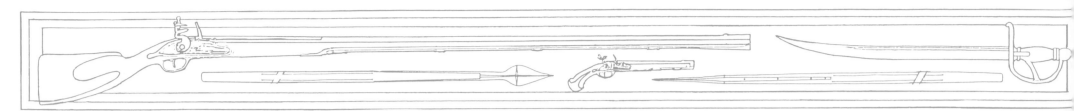

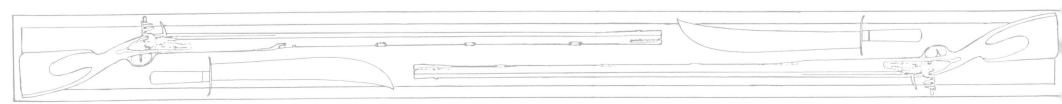

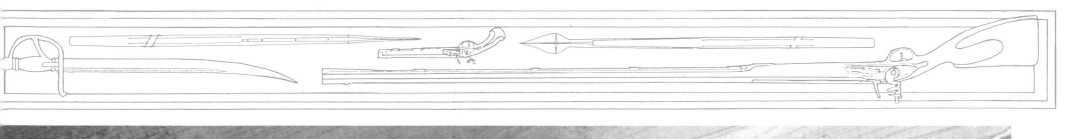

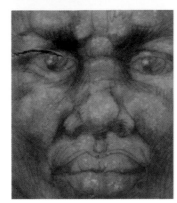

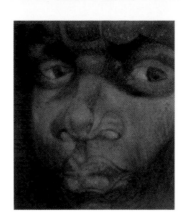

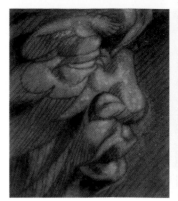

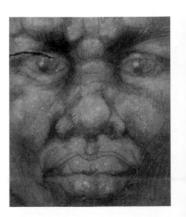

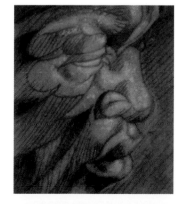

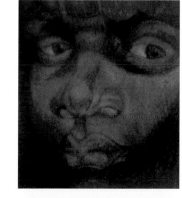

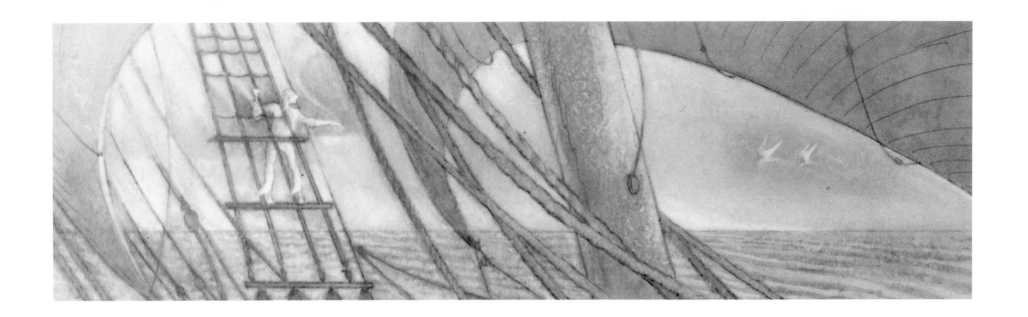

BIBLIOGRAPHY

Ottobah Cugoano. *Narrative of the Enslavement of Ottobah Cugoano, a Native of Africa.* http://docsouth.unc.edu/neh/cugoano/cugoano.html

Sylviane A. Diouf, ed. *Fighting the Slave Trade: West African Strategies.* Ohio University press, 2013.

Sylviane A. Diouf. *Dreams of Africa in Alabama: The Slave Ship Clotilda and the Story of the Last Africans Brought to America.* Oxford University Press, 2014.

David Eltis and David Richardson. *Atlas of the Transatlantic Slave Trade.* Yale University Press, 2015.

Olaudah Equiano. *The Interesting Narrative of the Life of Olaudah Equiano, or Gustavus Vassa, the African. Written by Himself.* http://docsouth.unc.edu/neh/equiano1/menu.html

Robin Law and Paul E. Lovejoy, eds. *The Biography of Mahommah Gardo Baquaqua.* Marcus Wiener Publishers, 2001.

Benjamin N. Lawrance. *Amistad's Orphans: An Atlantic Story of Children, Slavery and Smuggling.* Yale University Press, 2015.

Beverly C. McMillan, ed. *Captive Passage: The Transatlantic Slave Trade and the Making of the Americas.* Smithsonian Institution Press, 2002.

Marcus Rediker. *The Slave Ship: A Human History.* Viking, 2007.

Stephanie Smallwood. *Saltwater Slavery: A Middle Passage from Africa to American Diaspora.* Harvard University Press, 2007.

ACKNOWLEDGMENTS

There are so many people to acknowledge, too numerous to list, who played some part in this project directly or indirectly, whether they know it or not. People who helped set it in motion or kept it moving forward with their active encouragement, and those who waited patiently, and impatiently, for me to finish. All are important to me now. But for those who are no longer with us, who have passed on, yet whose spirits are still within me, I feel it is crucial and very important for me to name them. For to say their names, to remember them by repeating their names, is to keep them alive. I remember in my family my aunt Josephine Nash, my uncles Albert and Pollard Nash, and my father, Samuel Feelings. To my friends and mentors Elton Fax, John O. Killens, Charles White, Julian Mayfield, Ana Liva Mayfield, St. Clair Drake, George Wilson, Sara Lee, Sylvia Boone, Kofi Bailey, Alphaeus Hunton, Geri Wilson, Alice Childress, Romare Bearden, Shirley Graham DuBois, Owen Dodson, Simon Shulman, Melba Kgositsile, Don Lynn, and Dickie Robinson.

And to the living: my sons Zamani and Kamili. Trying to balance individual responsibility and collective responsibility, especially to the two of you, has been a struggle for me. I am sure too many times this struggle felt one-sided and seemed unfair because I wasn't there for you. But now, here in the present, I will take the time to build our relationships.

All this work could not have been published without some very important people working in the background. I thank my agent, Marie Brown, for doing what she does so well. Dr. John Henrik Clarke for bringing his volume of brilliant scholarship to the Introduction. And a special thanks for the talented touch of wordsmith Herb Boyd. And of course I thank my editor and publisher of over twenty-five years, Phyllis Fogelman, who has done more than her share of waiting for the completion of the artwork, and who has worked diligently and harmoniously with her art director, Atha Tehon, to produce a beautiful book. I thank you both again.

Finally, to all those wonderful ordinary, extraordinary people who have touched my life, from America to Africa, from Ghana to Guyana. Especially those of you who saw these images in progress and sometimes with your eyes, sometimes with your words, helped me to give this story back, in this form. I hope you all understand that your spirit lives within this book in the most positive way, even if your name is not listed here.

NKONSONKONSON
We are linked in both life and death. Those who share common blood relations never break apart.